IN THIS TOPZ ...

CU00947961

7350

Hello!!!

Welcome to this spectacularly special *Topz Tips for School*. It's packed full of helpful suggestions from our friends, the Topz Gang, and also amazingly wise words and advice from God's Word, the Bible.

Whether you're just starting a new class or school, or have been in the same one for a few years, we can help you find ways to make your school days the best they can be. From friendships to football, homework to holidays, bullying to behaving – it's all in here. And what's just the best is that we can tell God all about what's going on at school, and He promises to be there with us, to help and guide us along the way.

So keep this little book handy through good days and bad days – and see how God's love can really make a difference to every day at school.

Lynette

CWR

MIX
Paper from responsible sources
FSC® C015900

HOW TO USE Topz

The Bible books

Old Testament
Genesis
Exodus
Leviticus
Numbers
Deuteronomy
✦ Joshua
✦ Judges
Ruth
✦ 1 Samuel
2 Samuel
1 Kings
2 Kings
1 Chronicles
2 Chronicles
Ezra
Nehemiah
Esther
Job
✦ Psalms
Proverbs
Ecclesiastes
Song of Songs
Isaiah
Jeremiah
Lamentations
Ezekiel
Daniel
Hosea
Joel
Amos
Obadiah
Jonah
Micah
Nahum
Habakkuk
Zephaniah
Haggai
Zechariah
Malachi

New Testament
Matthew
Mark
✦ Luke
John
Acts
Romans
1 Corinthians
2 Corinthians
Galatians
Ephesians
Philippians
✦ Colossians
1 Thessalonians
2 Thessalonians
1 Timothy
2 Timothy
Titus
Philemon
Hebrews
James
1 Peter
2 Peter
✦ 1 John
2 John
3 John
Jude
Revelation

It may be that some of you haven't looked inside a Bible very much before. If so, here's a few helpful hints:

1 At the end of each topic in this *Topz* there's a Bible reading. It's shown like this:

Genesis
25 v 2-5

2

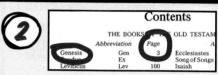

To find this, turn to the Contents page near the front of your Bible and look for the name of the **book** – which in the example is Genesis. Now find the **page** this book starts on and turn to it.

3 You will have to turn over a few pages now to get to the right **chapter**.

4 Now look for the **verse** numbers, which will be in smaller type. The **chapter** and **verse** will look like this:

Chapter **Verse**

5 After reading the Bible passage, go back to the *Topz* page and see what it says. Each Bible reading ends with a prayer too.

If you don't want to turn to the Contents page of your Bible all the time, you will see we've listed all the Bible books in order for you (see left). The ones you'll be reading from in this *Topz* are highlighted with a star ✦.

Use this *Topz* Marker to keep your place in *Topz*.
Cut it out and stick it to a piece of card to strengthen it.

GROWING UP
Are you ready?!

What's your favourite thing about going to school, John?

Erm ...

One of the things I like best is that it helps me to be more independent. I have to get up in good time in the mornings, get washed and dressed, have breakfast, and make sure I leave the house in plenty of time with everything I need. Mum helps, but I love getting myself organised.

I've just thought what my favourite thing about going to school is.

What?

The summer holidays ...

As you get older, people start wanting you to think for yourself more. And you're probably ready to be more independent, too.

You might start walking to school or to the bus on your own. You might have to make decisions – which topic am I going to choose? Which friend or group am I going to work with?

Growing more independent is very exciting, but it can be a little bit scary, too. Remember, we all need a little help now and then, and whose there to help you?
– Teachers!
– Parents or carers!
– And ... God! He's always ready to listen and He loves to hear from you.

3

Get organised!

Unless you're *really* good at leaping out of bed early in the morning, getting to school on time can sometimes turn into a bit of a rush.

TOPZ TIP

Don't leave getting everything ready till the morning - pack your bag the night before!

Here's a list of things you might want to check you have in your bag before you go to bed:

PENCIL CASE ✓
TEXT BOOKS ✓
HOMEWORK ✓
PE KIT ✓
READING BOOK ✓
LUNCH MONEY ✓
CALCULATOR ✓
EXERCISE BOOKS ✓

Can you find them all in the word search?

```
E W O D I P X E K y R I T
G X C A L C U L A T O R V
W H E F U E A y N X E E W
X V J R N N B L D P O A S
R P E N C I L C A S E D T
K D X E H I O U V H Q I A
C L E D M N S D R E M N V
P O B M O L B E R X K G B
E B H A N C O T B y M B E
K H O M E W O R K O U O S
I D O D y L K S M A O O N
T E A X T E X T B O O K S
A C L T H O M y T E K I S
```

When it comes to school, I try to be SUPER organised! I always try to put my **uniform** in the laundry basket when it's dirty. Same with my **PE kit**. I check my **pencil case** regularly to make sure my writing **pen**, a **pencil**, my **rubber**, **ruler** and **pencil sharpener** are in there. And before I go to bed, it helps if I put everything I'm going to need for the next day into my **school bag**.

Having a list is a good idea – it reminds me of anything I've forgotten, and as I put things in my bag I can tick them off the list.

Try making your own list and tick things off in the box once you've put them in your bag!

- ~~Ho reading book~~
- Journal
- Kindle
-
-
-
-
-
-

TOPZ TIP

Making a list is really helpful, especially at the end of the holidays. Topz all know that it takes a bit of effort getting back into the swing of things when term starts again!

GRAB YOUR BIBLE

Josie's Bible verse pick:
'Whatever you do, work at it with all your heart, as though you were working for the Lord'
(Colossians 3 v 23)

Have you ever had that 'I can't be bothered!' feeling?

Maybe you've been asked to tidy your bedroom. Or you have homework that needs to be done for tomorrow. Or it's Monday morning and you have to get up for school, but you just want to stay in bed!

When you really don't feel like doing something, it's easy to think, 'I can't be bothered!'

But there's never a second when God isn't bothered about you. He is with you every moment of every day. Ready to listen. Ready to help. God wants to give us His ALL – ALL the time! So let's give our ALL to Him.

Try your very best in everything you do. And keep on trying! God wants to see you learn and grow. Whatever work you have to do this week, do it as well as you can. **Be** bothered! Do everything as if you're doing it for God Himself!

PRAY

Dear God, thank You that You are always close beside me. Please help me to try my best at school and at home – every single day. Amen.

WHAT 'YA WORRIED ABOUT?!

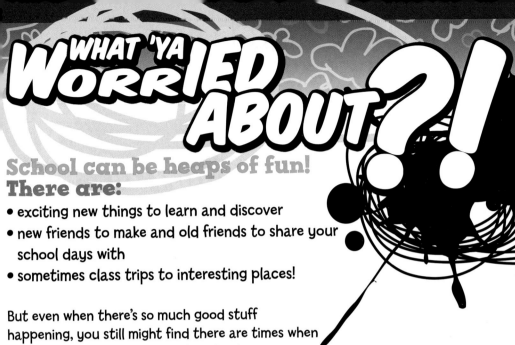

School can be heaps of fun! There are:

- exciting new things to learn and discover
- new friends to make and old friends to share your school days with
- sometimes class trips to interesting places!

But even when there's so much good stuff happening, you still might find there are times when you feel anxious about going to school.

Feeling anxious or worried - or even a bit scared about something - is really normal. Lots of people have feelings like that about lots of different things.

I'm scared of spiders. I hate it when I find them in the bath!

I get worried when I have to take a violin exam in case I play badly.

I feel anxious when I'm hungry and it's ages till lunch!

Don't let worries get you down

Doing something new can make people anxious and worried, too. So if you're starting at a new school or going into a new class it's only natural to feel nervous. You need time to get used to everything – new place, new teachers, new classmates.

Even when you've been at a school for a while, there may still be things you worry about. If there are, make sure you talk to someone about them – maybe a parent or teacher. Talk to your friends, too. They may be feeling just like you do.

And remember – God promises to be right beside you. Every single moment.

TOPZ TIP

1. Tell God how you feel.
2. Ask Him to help you to trust Him.
3. Give Him your fears and worries.
4. Know that He is with you every day and He will never leave you.

The Bible has some good advice about worry.
Follow the arrows to read what 1 Peter 5 v 7 says:
Start>

Leave

worries

all

him

cares

your

with

[God],

he

you.

because

for

God loves you and He wants to take away your worries so you can be happy at school.

GRAB YOUR BIBLE

Sarah's Bible verse pick:
'the LORD answered [Hannah's] prayer.'
(1 Samuel 1 v 19)

In the book of 1 Samuel, chapter 1, you can read about a woman called Hannah.

Hannah was very unhappy because she had no children. All she wanted was a baby. One day, she couldn't stand it any longer. She cried out to God. She told Him how sad she was. She begged Him for a baby. And at last, God answered her prayer. He gave Hannah a little baby boy and she called him, Samuel.

When Hannah was very unhappy, she didn't turn away from God. She turned **to** Him and she asked Him to help her. God listened. Then at the right time, He answered her prayer.

If something happens at home or at school to make you sad and upset, be like Hannah. Turn to God and tell Him how you feel. God may not always give us exactly what we want. He may not answer our prayers straightaway. But He **will** listen. And He **will** answer in the best way and at the best time.

Trust in God. He will never let you down.

PRAY

Thank You, Lord, that whenever I talk to You, and whatever I talk to You about, I know that You are always listening. Amen.

FRIENDSHIP TIPS!
Making Friends

Being in the Topz Gang is MEGA cool! And because we all go to the same school in Holly Hill, it means we get to see each other loads in term time as well as in the holidays. But I don't spend all my time at school just with Topz. At playtimes and lunchtimes, I like doing stuff with some of my other classmates, too. Especially playing football! I'll play football with anyone who asks me to!

That's true, he really will – even me and I'm rubbish at football!

Your class at school will most probably be made up of all sorts of girls and boys from all kinds of different backgrounds. Some of them may be a lot like you. Others may not be like you at all. But you are all in school to learn together – and every one of you will want to have friends.

TOPZ TIP

You might find that you enjoy having a group of friends (like the Topz Gang), or that you have a particular best friend. But having a few special friends doesn't mean that you can't be friendly with everyone else in your class, too. Just like Danny, it's good to try to get on with everybody.

Being at school isn't just about learning things from your teachers. It's about learning how to get on with others, too.

The more time you spend with your classmates, the more you will get to know them. You will find out who you can chat with easily, and who you really enjoy playing with. You'll discover who likes the same sorts of books and TV programmes that you like. You'll see who wants to spend time with you as much as you want to spend time with them.

The following words are topics you could ask a new friend about, to see what they like! Can you find them in the word search?

SPORT
SHOPPING
MUSIC
ART
READING
GAMES
PETS
CLUBS

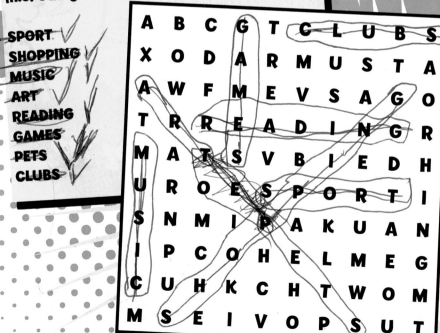

Falling Out

Sarah and me – we're the best friends ever.

We like the same things.

We laugh at the same jokes.

We do the same stuff.

But even WE fall out sometimes.

If I feel grumpy, I can get a bit snappy.

So can I.

And some days we might just argue about nothing at all!

But we always make up afterwards. Everyone gets cross sometimes. And when Sarah and I fall out, the most important thing we can do is to say sorry and forgive each other.

It can be hard to get on with everyone all the time – even with your best friends. Sometimes grumpy days just happen. But when you say sorry to God, He will always forgive you for doing or saying things that perhaps weren't very kind. And that's what He wants you to do, too – forgive other people.

TOPZ TIP

If you find it hard to forgive someone for upsetting you, ask God to help you so that you can be friends with them again.

Being a friend

When you start going to a new school or join a new class, what you really need are some classmates who will help you out and make you feel welcome. And when someone new comes into your class, that's what they need, too.

Think about how you would like your friends to treat you.

Now look at the list to the right. Put a tick beside the words that describe a good friend, and a cross beside the ones that don't. >>

Jesus, God's Son, is everything a good friend should be. Ask God to help you to grow more like Jesus so that you can be a good friend, too – not just to your best mates, but to everyone who needs a friend.

- ○ **kind**
- ○ **bad tempered**
- ○ **patient**
- ○ **loving**
- ○ **selfish**
- ○ **gentle**
- ○ **giving**
- ○ **mean**
- ○ **stubborn**
- ○ **helpful**

Your true best Friend

GRAB YOUR BIBLE

Danny's Bible verse pick:

'our love should not be just words and talk; it must be true love, which shows itself in action.'
(1 John 3 v 18)

God loves you in an amazing way.

He doesn't just love you if you do good things.
He doesn't just love you if you behave well all the time.
He doesn't just love you when you remember to talk to Him.
He doesn't just love you if you love Him back.

God loves you ALL THE TIME. And His love is TOTALLY UNSELFISH.

Think about your classmates. You'll have friends you get on with most of the time. You might have a particular best friend, too. Then there will be those you talk to sometimes. There may even be one or two who you don't really like.

What God hopes is that you'll try to be a good friend to everyone. Not just to your close friends. He wants you to learn to care for others the way He cares for you – totally unselfishly.

Think about all your classmates again now. **Does anyone need a friend?**

PRAY

Lord, thank You for being my best Friend. Please help me to be the best friend I can be. Amen.

RESPECT!

Playing by the RULES

While you're growing up, you might sometimes feel that your life is full of people and rules telling you what you *mustn't* do.

DON'T GO OUT IN THE RAIN WITHOUT A COAT.

DON'T WATCH TV UNTIL YOU'VE FINISHED YOUR HOMEWORK.

DON'T STAY UP LATE.

DON'T SPEAK TO STRANGERS.

DON'T PLAY FOOTBALL NEAR THE ROAD.

Ugh! What a lot of 'don'ts'! But I guess it's all pretty good advice ...

TOPZ TIP

Remember, your parents or carers want what's best for you! If they tell you not to do something, it's because they are trying to look after you, teach you good things and keep you safe. When you understand this, it's a lot easier to be respectful towards them and to the rules they set for you.

What about the teachers?

At school, it's your teachers who look after you. There are school rules to keep you safe and to help you to behave well and to respect each other.

Some teachers may be more 'shouty' than others, but they all want you to learn as much as you can while you are in their class. And they all want you to do well. Try to remember that when you're given homework you don't want to do!

Your teachers work very hard for you. They plan your lessons. They organise activities. They mark your work and keep an eye on how you're getting on.

They want to be encouraging and helpful. So it's very important to show them respect by being polite when you speak to them and by doing as they ask.

The Bible teaches us to treat others as we would like to be treated: 'Do for others what you want them to do for you' (Matthew 7 v 12).

TOPZ TIP

When you show respect to your teachers, you are obeying God.

> If I see one of my teachers with loads to carry, I ask if I can take something for them.

> When we have PE, I often help to put out the equipment.

> So do I!

Your teachers have lots to do and think about every day. Can you come up with some ways you could be helpful like Topz? It could be anything, from fetching stationery to holding a door open.

Have a think and write down your ideas here >>

Have you done your homework?!

As you get older, your teachers will start to give you work to do at home as well as in the classroom. And it can sometimes seem like a bit of a chore.

When you're given homework, you'll also be told when you need to have it finished and ready to hand in to your teacher. Most schools will give you a book to write homework tasks down in to remind you what you need to do. Make sure you always write down the hand-in dates as well.

However you feel about it, homework has to be done. So the best thing to do at the end of the school day or at the weekend is to get on with it FIRST, before you do anything else. That way, you'll be sure to give yourself plenty of time.

Not only that, but when your work is finished, you'll be able to relax and enjoy yourself much more knowing that you've already done what you need to do.

I don't usually mind doing my homework.

I always hate doing mine!

And guess what? Your teachers AND your parents will be much happier, too!

Obeying God

Dave's Bible verse pick:
'Joshua did as he was told.'
(Joshua 5 v 15)

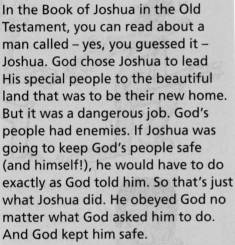

In the Book of Joshua in the Old Testament, you can read about a man called – yes, you guessed it – Joshua. God chose Joshua to lead His special people to the beautiful land that was to be their new home. But it was a dangerous job. God's people had enemies. If Joshua was going to keep God's people safe (and himself!), he would have to do exactly as God told him. So that's just what Joshua did. He obeyed God no matter what God asked him to do. And God kept him safe.

At school, you'll meet lots of people. Some of them may not think in quite the same way you do. They may have different ideas about what's right and what's wrong. Just remember that God is with you every day. He wants to take care of you, and He wants what is best for you.

So read your Bible and spend time talking to Him. The more you get to know Him, the more you will want to obey Him. Just like Joshua.

PRAY

Dear Father, thank You for loving me. Please help me to live my life the way that You want me to every day. Amen.

WHAT'S THE DEAL WITH BuLLYING?

Problems with bullying

Falling out with a friend is one thing. Hopefully you can talk to each other, sort the problem out quickly, and make up.

Bullying is something else. It's when one person, or a small group, picks on another in an unkind and cruel way. This can be through what the bully says: name-calling or nasty comments. Or it can be through what the bully does: spoiling or breaking something belonging to the person, and even hurting someone by pushing, hitting or kicking them. It can also involve ignoring them, or getting others to join in with the bullying, too.

And bullying doesn't just happen once. A bully might keep picking on someone – over and over again.

It is **NEVER** alright to pick on someone like this. Something must **ALWAYS** be done to STOP IT.

Why do some children get bullied?

It seems very unfair, but some children are more likely to get picked on than others. It might be:

- because of how they look, or
- because they are new to the school, or
- because they are shy and a bit quiet, or
- because they have a disability, or
- because they come from a different country
- or there may not be any obvious reason.

Being bullied makes children feel scared and alone. No one deserves to feel like this. If you notice someone being bullied, **NEVER JOIN IN**. Tell someone, like a parent or teacher, and see if you can find a time to talk to the person who is being picked on. They will need a friend.

And speak to God about it. God wants to help us with the little things and the BIG THINGS. Bullying is very serious. Remember that God is right beside you always.

He wants to hear from you. He wants to be involved in every part of your life.

Topz – here to help!

I've been bullied at school. I told my parents and everything's all sorted out now. I've been able to help a friend who was being bullied, too. If it ever happens to you, or you know someone who is being bullied, here are some important things to do …

ALWAYS tell someone – a teacher, your parents or a carer. Don't be scared to do this. If you think it'll be hard to talk to your parents, try writing everything down. Explain how being bullied makes you feel, too. Then give the note to your parents for them to read. The bully has to be stopped and they never need to know that it was you who told on them.

You could also tell someone else in your family – maybe a granny, auntie, older brother or sister – and ask them to talk to your parents for you. The main thing is that you TELL SOMEONE. Remember, your parents or carers don't want you to be bullied. As soon as someone knows about it, they can start to help make it stop.

TOPZ TIPS ON CYBERBULLYIN

Tell a good friend, too. Ask them to stick with you as much as they can through the day. If a bully is going to be nasty to you, it's more likely they'll do it if they catch you by yourself.

Try not to show that you're upset. If a bully thinks you're not bothered by them, they might get bored and give up.

Remember that bullies are human too, and it is very likely that they themselves are hurting in some way. So it can be hard not to, but don't answer back to a bully, and definitely don't hit back if someone has hurt you. It could only make matters worse and you might end up getting into more trouble. If something bad happens in school – GO AND TELL A TEACHER.

With all the chat and social websites there are, some people are being bullied online – this is called cyberbullying. Check out these Topz tips below.

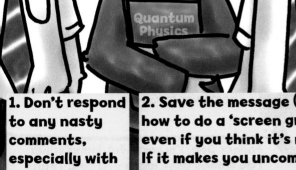

Quantum Physics

1. Don't respond to any nasty comments, especially with an equally mean response.

2. Save the message (ask someone how to do a 'screen grab/capture') even if you think it's not that bad. If it makes you uncomfortable or sad it's not right and it might be the start of bullying.

3. Show an adult as soon as possible.

God always forgives

GRAB YOUR BIBLE

Benny's Bible verse pick:
'let us celebrate with a feast! For this son of mine ... was lost, but now he has been found'
(Luke 15 v 23-24)

Benny's Bible verse comes from a story Jesus told to teach people about God's forgiveness:

A son leaves his father and moves out of the family home. But he is very foolish. He does wrong things and he wastes all his father's money – until he has nothing left at all. When he realises how stupid he has been, the son goes back to his father. He says he is sorry, but he doesn't expect his father to treat him like a son any more. So when his father shouts, 'Let's have a party to celebrate!' he probably has to stop himself falling over in surprise! The father forgives his son for everything. He is just so happy to have him home again.

God is like the father in Jesus' story. When we do wrong things, God is sad. Perhaps we have been caught up in bullying and lashed out at the bully or even bullied someone ourselves. But the good news is when we're really sorry and come back to God, He is always ready to forgive us.

So if you have a difficult day at school and end up saying or doing things you wish you hadn't, tell God you're sorry. Then KNOW that He forgives you because He loves you. And once you've been forgiven, then forgive others, too. Perhaps, if you have been bullied, think of that person now and forgive them. Give them over to God.

PRAY

Father God, I'm sorry for times when I do things that make you sad. Thank You for forgiving me and showing me how to forgive others. Please help me to live the way You want me to. Amen.

TOP MARKS!
Ready for a challenge?

School is all about learning new things. Some of them you will enjoy and find fairly easy. Others may seem harder and so you have to work at them more.

These are the lessons the Topz Gang like the most:

PE's the best.

PE for me, too!

I think I like everything.

I love English.

Not sure – but probably Art.

Definitely Maths.

Music – it's my favourite.

The Gang's favourites are the things they find easiest and are good at. But one of the challenges of school is to work especially hard at the subjects you may find more difficult. After all, it's important to understand and to learn how to do those things, too.

Lesson time!

WHICH ARE YOUR FAVOURITE SUBJECTS AT SCHOOL? WRITE THEM DOWN HERE:

english
topic
sicnce

IF YOU FIND ANY LESSONS HARD, WRITE THOSE DOWN TOO:

maths
~~topic~~
science

To help yourself as much as you can, always try to concentrate and listen carefully in lessons. Tell your teacher if you don't understand so that he or she can explain it to you again. And don't be afraid to make mistakes. Making mistakes is all a part of learning how to do new things. So don't give up. Just keep on trying.

Parents or carers, even older brothers and sisters, may be able to help you too. Chat to them about anything you are finding difficult at school. And talk to your classmates. They might understand something you don't.

Facing up to challenges in the classroom might be hard work, but it's always well worth the effort.

People who like to play sports tend to be quite competitive. They want to win – to be seen to be the best! There's nothing wrong with that. It's good to try hard in everything you do – as long as you're not unkind or unfair to anyone else along the way.

But it **isn't** good to feel miserable or really disappointed if something hasn't turned out the way you wanted it to. If you can, it's best just to shrug your shoulders and think, 'Oh, well, I'll try to do better next time'.

I got really cross with Danny once because he got picked for the Area Junior Football Squad and I didn't. But it was a stupid thing to get angry about. I still get to play football whether I'm in the Squad or not. And it was stonking when Danny and I made up again. Staying friends is way more important than worrying about who's better at what.

Priceless!

At school you may find that some of your classmates aren't just competitive when it comes to PE. They might try to be the best in the classroom, too.

Just as with sport, there's nothing wrong with trying your hardest in your other lessons. In fact, trying hard to learn new things is brilliant! But it can be easy to start comparing yourself with others when it comes to the marks you get for your work. If you find you have a talent for something and get good marks, don't boast about it. It's God who gives us our talents, so we need to try to remember to thank Him for them – not brag about them.

In the same way, if someone seems to be better at something than you, don't let it make you feel sad or not 'good enough'. People are good at different things. God made you EXACTLY as you are. And that's the way He loves you – EXACTLY as you are.

To God you are priceless. And you always will be.

Special to God

GRAB YOUR BIBLE

Paul's Bible verse pick:
'You created every part of me ... you saw me before I was born.'
(Psalm 139 v 13,16)

You are a one-off. Did you know that? A one-off creation with your own thoughts and ideas, your own skills and talents. You may be *like* someone else. But you will never be *exactly the same* as anyone else.

And guess what? That's just the way God planned it.

God loves seeing the world brimming full with different things! Look at all the different kinds of plants and trees there are. Think about all the different birds and animals. And as for the HUGE variety of insects and sea life – well – the mind boggles!

Differences are good and something to get excited about.

So learn to enjoy the differences you see between your classmates. And if ever anyone points the finger at you for being different and not like them, think: 'Good! God made me to be different and He loves my differences!'

God saw you before you were born. He made you exactly the way He wanted you to be. That's a perfect reason to hold your head high and say to yourself: 'I am special to God and I always will be.'

PRAY

Dear God, I praise You for making me just the way I am. Please help me never to forget how special I am to You. Amen.

WORK & PLAY

Benny, am I dull?

No, why?

'Cos there's that saying, 'All work and no play makes Jack a dull boy'. And I spend lots of time doing schoolwork 'cos I like it. Does that mean I'm boring?

No! It's good that you work hard. But it's important to take time off, too. You just have to make sure you do a bit of each.

Cool.

Er, Paul ...

Yeah?

Who's Jack ...?

God made us to be His friends. He also means us to work hard but to make sure we get lots of rest, too. God knows that, when we're busy, we need time to relax and do the things we like doing. Some people call it, 'recharging their batteries'.

So work hard at school. Get your homework done. But be sure to enjoy some time for yourself, too.

When I'm really busy, I make myself a timetable. It helps me work out how to fit everything I need to do into a day. And I feel better once I've written it all down.

HERE'S DANNY'S TIMETABLE FOR A BUSY FRIDAY IN TERM TIME.

7–8AM
Get up. Get washed and dressed. Have breakfast.

8AM
Read my Bible and pray.

8.30AM
Leave for school.

9AM – 3.30PM
At school.

4.30–5.30PM
Homework.

5.30PM
Dinner.

6PM
Youth club.

9PM
Prayer time and bed.

Danny's Friday is certainly very busy! But he's done two important things. He's made time for some fun and relaxation at youth club, and he's set aside some time to spend with God.

However long your list of things to do is, try to keep God at the very top! God loves you and wants what's best for you – and He looks forward to the times you spend with Him.

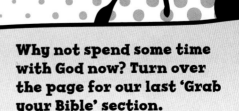

Why not spend some time with God now? Turn over the page for our last 'Grab your Bible' section.

GRAB YOUR BIBLE

God – right by your side

John's Bible verse pick:
'You can do it because I will help you.'
(Judges 6 v 16)

The book of Judges in the Old Testament tells the story of a man called Gideon.

Gideon was quite timid. To be honest, he was a bit of a scaredy cat. So he must have thought it was very odd when God said to him, 'Gideon! I want you to save my people from their enemies!' And odder still when God called him 'brave and mighty'!

But however Gideon felt about himself, God had a plan for him. And with God's help, Gideon made God's enemies run away.

In all the busyness of the school day, you might not think there's anything you can do for God. But if God wants you to do something, then you can be sure He will let you know.

He might speak to you through what you read in the Bible, or through what someone says to you, or through a feeling that you have. And He will always make you strong enough to do what He wants you to do.

God has a plan for your life, just as he had a plan for Gideon's. Look at today's verse again. God says: 'You can do it because I will help you.'
Seriously – wow!

PRAY

Thank You, Father, for the amazing plan You have for my life. I want to serve You always. Amen.

Answerz

Page 4:

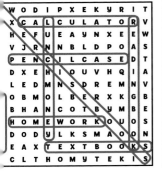

Page 11:

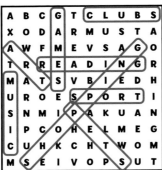

Page 13: A good friend is kind, patient, loving, gentle, giving and helpful – not bad tempered, selfish, mean or stubborn

Topz
Daily Bible notes

Have a great time reading the Bible and learning more about being God's friend.
- 72 pages
- Adventures with the Topz Gang
- Codes and puzzles
- Prayers and action ideas
- Features and competitions
- Your own Club pages

Topz
Guide to the Bible

You will find this the perfect start to becoming familiar with the Bible and appreciating the different exciting aspects of God's Word for you. The Topz Gang guide you through the Bible with:
- Colourful illustrations and cartoons
- Fun codes and puzzles
- Lots of information and action ideas

For current prices and to buy direct from CWR visit:
www.cwr.org.uk/topzbooks
or call 01252 784700.
Also available from Christian bookshops.

Here's a great way to
encourage 7- to 11-year-olds
at school, whatever stage
they're at ...

LOOK WHAT'S INSIDE ...

CARTOONS

PUZZLES

BIBLE READINGS

PRAYERS

... AND LOTS MORE!

From home to the classroom (and
the playground in between!),
Topz have got some brilliant tips
to help you make the most of
your school years! With relevant
Bible notes and a prayer at the
end of each topic, draw closer to
Jesus; your greatest Teacher
and best Friend.

CWR   www.cwr.org.uk

ISBN 978-1-78259-185-6

Written by Alexa Tewkesbury

CHILDREN'S BOOKS

You can get to know Jesus more and more with the regular edition of *Topz* which is published every two months. It is available from Christian bookshops, CWR or your National Distributor. See inside back cover for order form.

OTHER CWR DAILY BIBLE-READING NOTES
Every Day with Jesus for adults
Inspiring Women Every Day for women
Life Every Day (Jeff Lucas) for adults
Cover to Cover Every Day for adults
Mettle for 14- to 18-year-olds
YP's for 11- to 15-year-olds
Pens for 3- to 6-year-olds

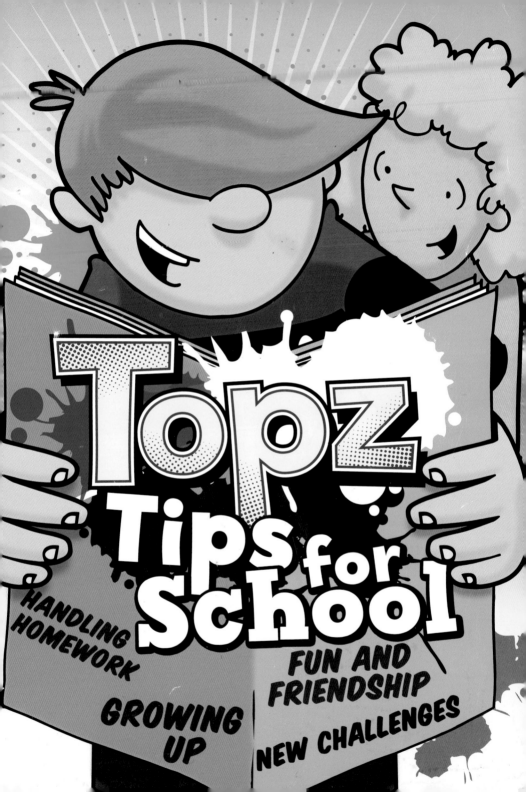